T0198903

ABC's of Surviving School Violence

written by
Natalie Johnson-Leslie and H. Steve Leslie
illustrated by Joshua Allen

AuthorHouse™
1663 Liberty Drive
Bloomington, IN 47403
www.authorhouse.com
Phone: 833-262-8899

Because of the dynamic nature of the Internet, any web addresses or links contained in this book may have changed since publication and may no longer be valid. The views expressed in this work are solely those of the author and do not necessarily reflect the views of the publisher, and the publisher hereby disclaims any responsibility for them.

Any people depicted in stock imagery provided by Getty Images are models, and such images are being used for illustrative purposes only.
Certain stock imagery © Getty Images.

This book is printed on acid-free paper.

ISBN: 978-1-4490-6397-9 (sc)

Library of Congress Control Number: 2010901093

Print information available on the last page.

Published by AuthorHouse 06/16/2022

authorHOUSE®

Dedication

This book is dedicated to the many families whose lives have been impacted directly or indirectly by school violence. Additionally, we dedicate this book to our children Gabrielle and Daniel; as well as their grandmothers Imogene Johnson and Silvin Leslie.

Acknowledgement

The authors wish to acknowledge the following individuals and organizations who contributed to this book: Arkansas State University (A-State) Police Department Childhood Services; Departments of Teacher Education and Communications; and a wide variety of parents and teachers. Our sincere gratitude goes to the children who participated in the focus group discussions; Alex and Brandon Solórzano, Donna and Ruth Morara, and Lucy Mokua. These children were inspirational in helping the authors understand the impact of school violence from their perspective. It was refreshing to have these children guide us in the early phase of compiling the manuscript.

Special thanks to Dr. Rob Lamm, Associate Professor in the Department of English and Philosophy at A-State for providing feedback in developing the final manuscript. It is with heartfelt thanks that we say thank you all for helping us communicate such vital information with the hope that the incidences of school violence may be greatly reduced and eventually eradicated from our society.

So listen little children to what I say
Don't be violent night or day
Violence in school is always wrong
We must be kind to everyone

C = Call 911 then silence the phone

D = Do not huddle in a group— spread far to be alone

E = Exercise caution when you hide

F = Flip off the light switch and watch from every side

I = If you hear a loud bang; Stop! Drop! and make no sound

J = Jump if you must— keep close to the ground

K = Kick if you can to be protected from harm

DO NOT TOUCH !

L = Look left, look right; do not touch the fire alarm

FIRE ALARM PULL DOWN

M = Move quickly away from violent actions

N = Non-violence leads to satisfaction

O = Officers are on their way to keep you out of danger

P = Prepare to remain under-cover like a ranger

S = Show your hands to the officer and spread your fingers wide

T = Time to tell what you saw—
no more need to hide

V = Violence is wrong;
it can make you so afraid

W = Watch for the safety of
others—this is expected

X = eXtra kindness is needed and will not be rejected

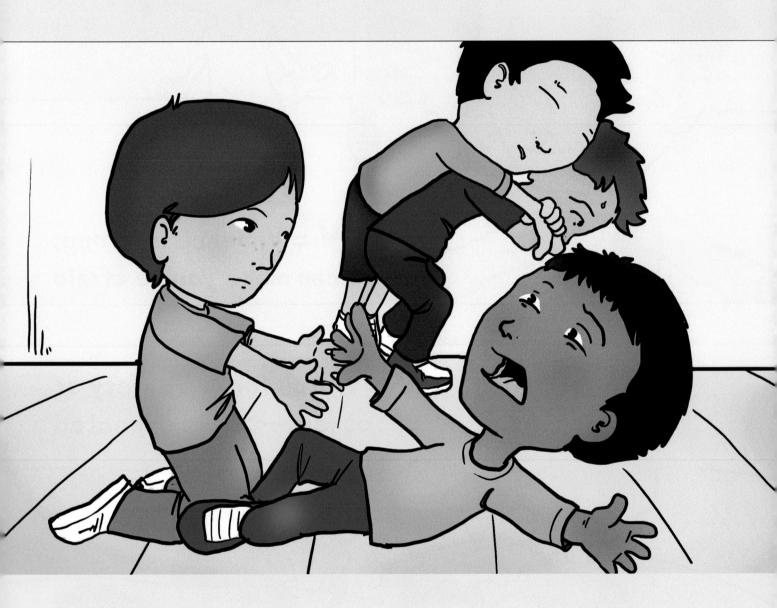

Y = YUCK! Being violent is not nice; being violent is not cool

Z = Zoom in on surviving violence if it happens at your school

So listen little children to what I say
Don't be violent night or day
Violence in school is always wrong
We must be kind to everyone

Epilogue

The issue of school violence continues to be of concern to parents, teachers, administrators, and the public at large. How knowledgeable are young kids about possible options to survive an incident of violence in their classroom, lunchroom, library, or on the playground? At what age is it appropriate to teach young kids safety tips about school violence? In schools, young kids are taught safety features in case of fires, tornadoes, and strangers. Unfortunately, the majority of the incidents of school violence are not perpetuated by strangers. What can be done to fill this gap? In spite of more security in schools, school violence continues to plague our society.

Today, school systems at all levels from day-care centers to universities continue to suffer the pain and loss of many members of their communities through the cold hands of school violence. Those most affected by the plague of school violence are families who lose loved ones. Thus, it makes sense that surviving school violence should be addressed head on from a young age when young minds can be influenced to make the right choices. The message presented in this book is an attempt to educate, inform and emphasize, practical, common-sense principles and practices that can save lives in the event of school violence. Parents and teachers can use this book to supplement early learners' introduction to the alphabet with survival tips to overcome violent acts. This way one fewer life may be lost through school violence because of the knowledge shared with early learners in this book.

Printed in the United States
by Baker & Taylor Publisher Services